# THE ROSE GARDEN

Tea Roses

ELVIN McDONALD

# THE ROSE GARDEN

*Tea Roses*

SMITHMARK

ELVIN McDONALD

This edition published by Smithmark Publishers, a division of U.S. Media Holdings, Inc., 115 West 18th Street, New York, NY 10011.

Smithmark books are available for bulk purchase for sales promotion and premium use. For details, write or call the manager of special sales, Smithmark Publishers, 115 West 18th Street, New York, NY 10011.

TEXT & PHOTOGRAPHY: Elvin McDonald
DESIGN: Stephen Fay
SERIES EDITOR: Kristen Schilo, Gato & Maui Productions

Printed and bound in Hong Kong

10 9 8 7 6 5 4 3 2 1

ISBN 0-7651-9064-8

Library of Congress
Cataloging-in-Publication Data

McDonald, Elvin.
    Tea roses / Elvin McDonald.
        p. cm.
    ISBN 0-7651-9064-8 (alk. paper)
    1. Hybrid tea roses.    I. Title.
SB411.65.H93M34    1998
635.9´33734–dc21                    98-18879
                                                    CIP

DEDICATION

Teas
for Ron and red roses

Lyn and roses
for the Governor's mansion

*Thanks especially
to Carol Hendrick of Brenham, Texas,
for helping edit the pictures at the outset,
to Hilary Winkler of San Francisco,
my research assistant,
who helped sort the words at the end,
to Dave Kvitne,
who actually dug the beds
and planted the roses in my garden...
and
to the gardeners
who permitted me to photograph
in their gardens...*

✹

*Tea Roses* and its three sibling books from *The Rose Garden* series, *Climbing Roses, Shrub Roses,* and *Old-Fashioned Roses,* have their beginnings in the first rose I planted at age five, about fifty-five years ago, but most specifically in the season (1985) when it was my privilege to work for days and weeks alongside world-class rosarian Stephen Scanniello in the Cranford Rose Garden at the Brooklyn Botanic Garden. Later, I grew and sold roses in Houston, Texas, and I am now in the process of planting my own rose garden in West Des Moines, Iowa. Book teammates, publisher Marta Hallett, series editor Kristen Schilo, and designer Stephen Fay, helped make my *Color Garden* series, *Red, White, Blue,* and *Yellow,* an international success. *The Rose Garden* series is written in the same spirit, to say the big things about a complex subject in a small book.

# Contents

# Beginnings

**THINK BACK MORE THAN A CENTURY,** to the years leading up to 1867: Hybrid perpetuals and teas were the roses of the time until that moment in Lyons at the nursery of Jean-Baptiste Guillot when "something different" was noted about one of the seedlings. Presumed to be a natural hybrid between a hybrid perpetual and a tea, it was destined to be the first recognized hybrid tea and christened 'La France.'

What was "different" was that it was a tidy, upright plant that produced buds packed with petals. In turn, these opened into the high-centered roses equated, to this day, with classic shape and exhibition conformation.

"Tea" will always be one of the most romantic names attached to the rose. Originally called tea-scented China roses, they were thought to smell either of tea leaves or of the tea crates in which they arrived, imported from Asia to England in the early 19th century. Today's noses mostly smell roses, not tea, but everyone agrees, the buds that are beginning to open make perfect boutonnieres.

**AT LEFT:**
'La France,' the first hybrid tea, introduced in 1867, continues to be grown for its exquisite form and classic rose fragrance.

**ABOVE & FAR LEFT:**
'Queen Elizabeth,' the first grandiflora, was introduced in 1955. Possessed of slight tea fragrance, everything else about this rose is larger than life; it is an all-time great.

*Beginnings*

AT LEFT: 'Sombreuil,' one of the hardiest tea roses, also a recurrent bloomer, dates from 1850. It exudes tea fragrance and is ideal for training on arbors and fences.

## 'MAMAN COCHET' LIVES!

THE BUDS *of this 1893 introduction are said to epitomize the modern long-budded rose. It is also the source of true orris fragrance, an aroma forever linked with scented linens and potpourris found in the finest homes of the South and West. As a rule, the tea roses are said to be hardy as far north as New York City or possibly Philadelphia. This suggests Zone 6 gardens in protected spots and almost anywhere in Zone 7 or warmer.*

*'Mrs. Dudley Cross' (1907) is one of the hardiest teas in cultivation, particularly in drier climates. Since the buds pack so many petals, they can balk in overly wet and rainy weather.*

*The tea roses as a class can be counted on in the South, for pink, yellow, crimson, or cream flowers and lots of fragrance.*

The legend of the "tea" rose lives on—for the true tea roses are in fact excellent, carefree flowering shrubs for warmer-climate gardens. Elsewhere, they adapt well to growing in big pots that can be wheeled to a protective place to avoid any fatal deep freezes that could occur.

One of the oldest, 'Bon Silene,' existed prior to 1837. 'Safrano,' dating from 1839, is said to be the first offspring gained by controlling parentage through hand pollination. 'Perle des Jardins' (1890) in its climbing form is a current favorite, itself descended from what was once the most important yellow greenhouse rose grown for the florist trade.

It would be nearly a hundred years before the first grandiflora would make its appearance, and an extraordinary and enduring rose it is: Christened 'Queen Elizabeth,' it was the creation of America's Walter Lammerts, All-America Rose Selection (AARS) in 1955. Every stem makes a bouquet.

The big, silvery pink flowers have classic hybrid tea shape and emit old-fashioned "tea" fragrance. The bushes are strong enough for hedges and backgrounds. Most amazing for the time was a large-flowered hybrid rose that produced bunches of blooms originating from a single point. Before 'Queen Elizabeth,' this trait had been associated with smaller polyanthas and floribundas.

Guillot's 1881 tea 'Etoile de Lyon' is everything a tea rose can be, pro and con: color, form, and fragrance get high marks despite their misfortune to be borne by weak, twiggy growth.

The official golden-yellow also fades by high noon on a hot day, to the cool paleness of a gardenia. No rose could be finer for a bud vase or mixing in a bouquet with other flowers. The fact that a rose introduced more than a hundred years ago survives despite certain physical weakness speaks volumes to the all-around satisfaction of growing 'Etoile de Lyon' and any true tea rose.

'Duchesse de Brabant' is cold-hardy in the relatively warm Zones 7 to 9. It blooms continuously and, along the Gulf Coast, continues after a century and a half to be one of the most-loved roses. In Zones 6 and colder, it can be grown in an 18-inch or larger pot that can be placed outdoors in warm weather or inside a greenhouse in the winter.

'Hallmark' hybrid tea came from American breeder Dennison Morey in 1966 and is generous in flower and fragrance from beginning to end of the season. Its family tree is rich in big red roses that are perfume factories, in the garden and cut, including 'Chrysler Imperial' and 'Oklahoma.' 'Hallmark' opens as a high-centered exhibition flower, then ages to a full-blown beauty.

## HYBRID PERPETUALS

LONG BEFORE *there were hybrid tea roses there were hybrid perpetuals. Though they continue, these roses had their start in the 1830s and are forever linked with Victoriana. Jules Laffay's 'La Reine' or 'Reine des Français' from 1842 is possibly the oldest of the lot still in cultivation —a treasure with its high centered buds that transform into fat, cupped roses.*

*Nearly half the roses listed in an 1882 book of 1,000 varieties were hybrid perpetuals. It is believed that as many as 4,000 were named and in commerce by the end of the 19th century, to be almost immediately eclipsed by their progeny, the almighty hybrid tea.*

*A favorite in cultivation is 'Baronne Prevost,' a contemporary of 'La Reine,' but from the French breeder Desprez. A strong to five feet shrub rose, it produces a dependable, if intermittent showing of large, rose-pink, and fragrant flowers on thorny, vigorous canes worthy of impenetrable hedging. This also works well as a specimen in a shrub border or as background for perennials.*

*The hybrid perpetuals extant today are hardy almost everywhere in the continental U.S. They need cutting back to size in early spring; some of the oldest, bloomed-out canes removed to the ground annually; and may give a better performance if pegged, to force lateral budding.*

The terms used to define roses change from time to time in order to reflect new ideas about their culture and use in the landscape, as well as developments in bush or flower habit. While old tea roses and hybrid perpetuals remain firmly placed under those labels, more recent creations, particularly hybrid teas and grandifloras, have now been reduced to a single category: large-flowered hybrid.

It is the "tea" connection that lends romance to the lot and the reasonable expectation that any big, beautiful rose probably will smell like a genuine "tea" rose and that it must therefore also be related. Of course, not all teas are fragrant and those that are run the gamut of smells attributed to roses. Everyone will agree, the vision of a long-stemmed, large-flowered, exhibition rose is a peaceful one, bearing the genteel civility of an afternoon tea in the company of friends.

AT RIGHT, ABOVE: The beautiful 'Scarlet Queen Elizabeth' is slightly fragrant and relatively thornless. It came out to acclaim in 1963.

AT RIGHT, BELOW: Hybrid perpetual roses reached their zenith during the reign of Queen Victoria, 1837-1901. They are hardy, remontant, and first-rate garden plants.

While the original tea roses are not very cold hardy, it is beneficial to remember their legacy—the large-flowered hybrids, the hybrid teas, and grandifloras, can grow in Zones 4 through 9 with hilling-up or other appropriate protection.

# *Excellence*

**TO BE THE BEST OF THE BEST,** a rose must achieve an all-around excellence that prevails wherever and by whomever it is grown. Out of every year's crop of hopefuls, some will go on to become classics; most however, will disappear from commerce after several seasons, or become cult favorites.

Part of the magic lies in matching the character and color of the rose to a name with which it resonates. 'Mister Lincoln' is a statuesque rose with a courageous red color. 'Dainty Bess' addresses the simplicity of a single, five-petaled, wild-rose flower with a childlike penchant for revealing its golden stamens. When it was time for a rose to be named in her honor, Rosie O'Donnell requested pure white. 'Rosie O'Donnell' the rose (by Tom Carruth, 1998), taps into her gregarious television persona, a Look at me! What are you going to do about it? red-and-white bicolor with pizzazz to go.

It is always fun to see for whom the new roses are named each year, and to offer a special place to those that honor our heroes and heroines.

AT LEFT: 'Dainty Bess' is considered the best all-around single hybrid tea, favored by untold gardeners (and bees) since its introduction in 1925. The modestly scented flowers appear in generous clusters, outstanding in the garden or bouquets.

17

AT LEFT: 'Gold Medal,' a 1982 grandiflora, is one of the best all-around yellows. It has a light tea scent. BELOW, LEFT: 'Elina,' also known as 'Peaudouce,' is a 1984-85 hybrid tea of slight fragrance, but a super producer of pale yellow and ivory flowers. BELOW RIGHT: 'King's Ransom,' a 1961 hybrid tea, has a sweet, fruity fragrance and continues to define the best of the best in modern yellow roses. Its long, pointed buds open slowly into large flowers that stand up well in all kinds of weather. Upright habit and long stems suit it to a tall bud vase or for lavish arrangements.

AT RIGHT, OPPOSITE: 'Midas Touch' is a 1994 hybrid tea and an All-America Rose Selection. The non-fading neon yellow flowers yield a fruity fragrance and reach their biggest size in cool weather.

The fabled "yellow rose of Texas" grew out of a song, not literally from the ground. The expression is said to refer in life to a real woman. So powerful are the imagery and spirit of the words and music, that all yellow roses are the beneficiaries of good public relations and positive brand identification. In other words, we are predisposed to liking almost any yellow rose we see.

Any modern yellow rose will have in its lineage at least one of the four "stud" roses that arrived in England from China. In this case it is the fourth "stud" rose that came in 1824. Known unofficially as "Park's Yellow Tea-scented Rose," the Royal Horticultural Society would soon give it the official name *Rosa odorata*  'Ochroleuca.' "Park's Yellow" imparted in its progeny the delightful trait of remontancy, that is, to bloom repeatedly through the season, and to have the coveted "tea" scent.

Breeding work done by Pernet-Duchet around 1890 in France was also to have a lasting effect on large-flowered, yellow, everblooming roses. Although he might be remembered alone for creating 'Mme. Caroline Testout,' a glorious big pink rose that remains popular today in its climbing form, or for florist roses that were the toast of their times, his greatest achievement is thought to be 'Soleil d'Or,' a hybrid tea introduced in 1900. A cross between 'Antoine Ducher' (a red hybrid perpetual) x *R. foetida persiana* (introduced into Europe from S.W. Asia in 1837), it brought bright, brassy yellow firmly into the lineage of what are today known generically as modern, large-flowered, yellow roses. Besides those pictured, some recent ones include 'Sun Goddess' (light scent), 'Gina Lollobrigida' (heady fragrance), 'Marco Polo' (spicy), and 'Golden Eagle' (honoring the bald eagle), which resists fading in hot weather, and has light fragrance.

These roses look beautiful alone, in a single bouquet, or mixed with something heavenly like blue delphiniums or sky-blue pansies.

Pure and pristine, white large-flowered roses are favored for weddings, and the all-white or Alba garden. This can lead to a small confusion since there is a distinct class of roses known as the Albas. It is an old class, known at least since the Middle Ages. The Albas are thought to descend from natural crosses between the dog rose, *Rosa canina*, and *R. x damascena* or *R. gallica.*

There are around a dozen Albas in cultivation, ranging from pure white through pastel pinks to bright rose-pink. All are grandly fragrant, among the easiest to grow of the old roses, and none is remontant. Among the whites are the "White Rose of York" (*R. x alba*), 'Blanche Superbe' (1817), 'Maxima,' 'Mme. Plantier,' 'Pompon Blanc Parfait' (an 1876 introduction and therefore the newest), and 'Semi-plena.'

Favorite and best-of-best modern white, everblooming, large-flowered roses include 'Pascali,' 'White Lightnin',' 'Victorian Lace,' 'John F. Kennedy,' 'Caroline de Monaco' (cream), 'Honor,' and 'Mt. Hood.' A recent entrant in the class, 'Fountain Square,' has exceptional vigor and the good habit of non-stop production of exhibition flowers. The latest is 'Grand Finale,' a big, white-ivory flower with light, honeysuckle fragrance over basic rose.

**ABOVE:** 'White Lightnin' is a 1981 grandiflora that blooms profusely and gives off an amazing amount of lemon-fresh fragrance. The rounded, medium-size bushes clothe themselves with glossy, bright green leaves. Every vigorous stem becomes a virtual bouquet that is long-lasting in the garden or cut to brighten the house.

'Pascali,' introduced in 1969, is always on the short list for Best White Hybrid Tea. It is an offspring of a cross of grandiflora 'Queen Elizabeth' x hybrid tea 'White Butterfly.' Lightly tea-scented, cream-suffused white exhibition flowers stand on sturdy erect stems above semi-matte, dark green foliage.

AT RIGHT: 'Olympiad' is a 1984 hybrid tea with light fruity scent from the reddest of red, medium-large flowers.
BELOW, LEFT: 'Red Masterpiece' is a 1974 hybrid tea with big flowers and true rose fragrance to match.
BELOW, RIGHT: 'Mister Lincoln,' a 1965 hybrid tea, always dazzles with its velvety color and rich, old damask rose scent.

Being red is no big deal if you're a rose, after all, the family name Rosa traces directly to age-old words used to express the color red. A current dictionary says that rose as a color is "purplish red, pinkish red, light crimson." Another source describes red as "a primary color" or any of a "spread at the lower end of the visible spectrum,... blood to pale rose or pink."

Within these two color descriptions lies at least one clue as to what helps define a red rose as great: the code words are "purplish" and "blood," the latter a liability if "bluish." A common human response to a purplish or bluish-red rose, it seems, is to feel it speaks of death and melancholy. Add a tweak of yellow and the mortuary chill turns to a cheery, straight-forward, stimulating "red," in reality perceived differently, depending on the eyes and temperament of the beholder. A pure rose-pink rose such as 'Timeless' (1997 AARS) has blue in it, the hopeful sort of blue associated with fair-weather skies.

AT LEFT: 'Olympiad' holds true red from the bud stage to the spent flower. With 'Ingrid Bergman' it is a parent of the 1998 red, red 'Opening Night.'

Two 1998 AARS winners are large-flowered, red roses, 'Opening Night' (clear crimson aging to deep pink, hybrid tea) and 'Fame!' (a raspberry-red, grandiflora).

When it comes to matching roses to names, 'Peace' is the all-time definitive example. Introduced in 1945, at the end of devastating world wars, anyone still living would welcome the promise of an indescribably beautiful rose named 'Peace.' If Guillot sensed something "different" about that first hybrid tea, so too must have Francis Meilland when he began to realize that number 3-35-40 in his stud book was looking bigger and better than anything known. As it happened, the rose would travel under different names around the world—'Madame A. Meilland,' 'Joy,' 'Gloria Dei'—but on the day it was christened 'Peace' in America, Sunday, April 29, 1945, at a gathering of rose lovers in Pasadena, California, by curious coincidence, Berlin also fell.

Later, on the day 'Peace' was declared an All-America Rose Selections winner, the war in Japan ended. A month later, again on dates fixed far in advance, the American Rose Society gave its supreme gold medal to 'Peace' even as the peace treaty was signed in Japan.

Though Francis Meilland would die young, he left the legacy of 'Peace' in the able hands of his wife Luisette and their children Alain and Michéle. A half a century later it is hardly possible to visit any rose breeder's trial grounds and fields without hearing the often-mentioned observation that in so many words says, "This rose is looking unusually strong or beautiful," (therefore implied), "it must have 'Peace' in its blood."

A most famous offspring, 'Chicago Peace' is a sport identical to 'Peace' except for color: everything about 'Peace' in form and stature, except the usual primrose and pink turned up to shimmering copper and orange. It appeared spontaneously in a man name Johnston's backyard. Imagine his surprise and delight.

**AT LEFT:** 'Chicago Peace,' a 1962 sport of 'Peace,' is a rosarian's dream.

**THIS PAGE:** 'Peace' in all stages is arguably the most beautiful large-flowered hybrid rose ever created. Lightly scented, it came from the Meilland family in France in 1945.

CLOCKWISE FROM ABOVE: 'Shining Hour' is a 1991 grandiflora with a light, fruity fragrance. It is an ideal bush rose for bedding as well as cutting. 'Camelot' is a 1965 grandiflora with spicy clove fragrance and high petal count (45-50) in a very double flower that opens slowly from glorious, long-stemmed buds. 'Tournament of Roses' earned AARS distinction in 1989, a grandiflora with a light, spicy scent. 'Yankee Doodle' is a 1976 hybrid tea with up to 70 petals that open into huge flowers exuding a light tea perfume and are extremely satisfying to grow. 'Shreveport' is a 1982 grandiflora with light scent. Long stems make it ideal for cutting.

All-around excellence tends to assure a rose's perpetuation and availability, although not necessarily. No one grower could possibly maintain and supply all the roses known to cultivation. If the cultivar you want is not available locally, check the catalogs of specialists; names and addresses are included under Resources.

A standard reference for determining a rose's general merits is the annually published ratings list from the American Rose Society. It's the familiar 0 to 10 rating system, with 9.0 and higher being a rose that has delivered on time and up to standards in a variety of climates all over the North American continent.

In the final analysis, the best rose for you will be the one that grows most beautifully on the conditions you are comfortable supplying. Success is the only option when planting a rosebush; failure a remote possibility unless nothing is planted. Bare-root bushes are shipped and set to grow primarily in early spring. Containerized roses, often in bloom, are available locally for planting any time the ground can be worked.

There is no mystery about growing roses. They need at least a half day of sun, well-drained soil, water during dry weather, and occasional deadheading.

## MULCHING IS MORE THAN A COSMETIC TREATMENT

R**OSES HAVE** *a way of looking neater and growing better if they are set off by an organic mulch and the bed is defined by being raised or mounded. In this framework, the rosebush stands out and also benefits from the moisture and temperature stablizing effects of the mulch and the drainage and root aeration provided by a raised bed.*

*If any mulch used is not already well-rotted or decomposed, a mulch made of bark chips, for example, it will be necessary to apply a time-release fertilizer to "feed" the bark as it begins to rot and break down, otherwise the roses could be robbed and become chlorotic.*

*Side-dressing bushes in late autumn or early winter, after the soil freezes, using compost or well-rotted manure, is highly beneficial, but avoid piling directly on top of a bush. By spring, this will have broken down, possibly to a dark, fertile color, that after raking proves sufficiently uniform to serve as mulch.*

# *Fragrance*

**TAKE TIME TO SMELL THE ROSES** has entered everyday language as a metaphor for taking joy in the moment. Of course, not all roses are fragrant, yet the accepted idea of the rose is of a full-petaled blossom that is redolent with the essence of true rose. "True" rose? Depending on the nose, the rose, the sensitivity to smell, different experiences are possible from the same blossom. Almost always there is something undeniably "rose" that underlies all the other nuances of scent that come when first smelling a flower. It may be all rose or a combination including citrus, orange-blossom, violet, raspberry, or "fruity."

Fragrance is often most active in the morning, as the sun comes out, dries off the dew, and its warmth begins to volatilize the myriad of oily essences that take to the air as delightful vapors.

An unusual way to intensify the experience of a garden redolent with the smell of roses is to edge the walkways with a variety of different rose-scented geraniums. They are entirely compatible with rosebushes. Brushing their foliage in passing releases "true rose" from a pelargonium leaf!

AT LEFT: 'Double Delight' has set a new standard for fragrance in modern roses. AT RIGHT: From the time they can walk, children seem compelled to smell the roses.

28

LEFT: 'Blue Moon' is one of the bluest roses and very fragrant. BELOW, LEFT: 'Sheer Bliss' has spicy fragrance. BELOW, RIGHT: 'Tiffany' is highly perfumed and a gifted, all-around performer. RIGHT, ABOVE: 'Sweet Surrender' has a heavy tea rose fragrance. RIGHT, BELOW: 'John F. Kennedy' has a licorice scent.

All roses aren't always fragrant, yet myth has it that all the old roses were and not one of the new ones is. Apparently, this is because those roses having the trait have been historically more likely to be kept in cultivation. In over a century of intense breeding, many of the large-flowered hybrid roses to come on the scene have continued to carry among them all the old familiar fragrances.

Recent awareness of the benefits of aromatherapy has refocused interest on the need for fragrance in any new roses introduced into cultivation. An early writer on the joys and benefits of the gardening lifestyle, Alice Morse Earle, commented that often after placing a bouquet of fresh-cut, fragrant roses in her room, she would notice that a nagging headache had completely disappeared. If we are sensitive to its possible benefits, rose fragrance will always possess this powerful aromatherapy healing potential.

So powerful the appeal of rose fragrance, the latest catalog from Jackson & Perkins lists not a single large-flowered rose that isn't fragrant. In fact, almost every rose-miniatures, landscape, old, and new roses that look old—all have fragrance. Adding to the appeal is the range of scent—which might suggest "raspberry," "newly mowed grass," or "clean, fresh."

ABOVE: 'Confidence,' from the Meillands of France, 1951, emits a delicate perfume, with discretion as the name implies. ABOVE, RIGHT: 'Brandy,' from the Americans Swim and Christensen in 1981, won AARS the next year and has ever after been an all-time favorite for color and strong tea scent. AT RIGHT: 'Kordes Perfecta,' from Wilhelm Kordes of Germany, 1957, is the sort of rose that if entered in an international competition would most likely earn high 9s and 10s in all events except fragrance: here rating takes a fall, for being "moderately" fragrant.

If you would like to increase your pleasure and awareness of fragrance in roses, try staging a rose-smelling (like a wine tasting) with some of your friends. For best results, you'll need a lush garden with at least a dozen different blooms and labels so you can set up a blind test. You could stage it as part of a Saturday or Sunday brunch or for an early evening garden party.

Ask each person to consider the smell they get from a rose on first impression and to write a brief, but vivid, description of it.

It may be "rosy" or "like lemon," "with hints of violet," or the disappointing, "nothing." Some roses are fragrant except when we try to smell them, or so it seems, and quite possibly some roses are never giving of any fragrance the human nose can perceive or appreciate.

The "fruity" smell attributed to certain roses is no joke, but refers to their kinship with all the other members of the rose family, including apple, quince, cherry, apricot, and raspberry. If you are asked to name that smell in a rose and it reminds you of any or all of these fruits, don't be surprised. And if one doesn't come to mind right away, "fruity" can only add bonus points to the rose's rating.

Or maybe after all, you will smell the elusive "tea" of rose lore.

## ROSE VOWS

'HONOR' *(left) 1980, and its hybrid tea sibling 'Love,' came from America's William Warriner in 1980, along with the inevitable if floribunda 'Cherish.' No one ever said they were anything more than moderately, mildly, or slightly fragrant. Yet their appearance as a trio with names synonymous with romance inspired a new interest in big, beautiful roses that if fussed over a bit might win in competition or at the very least take your breath away. In 'Love,' the contrast between the scarlet-red petals inside and its frosty outside dramatizes the form and every curve of a true exhibition-style tea rose. 'Cherish,' a floribunda, grows clusters of coral-pink classic high-centered flowers on a strong bush that responds well to frequent cutting for bouquets, if fortified each time with additional water and fertilizer and reasonably tolerable growing weather.*

**ABOVE, LEFT:** The glowing orange-copper 'Tropicana' took the eyes by storm when it came onto the garden scene in 1963, and there was enough vaguely raspberry scent to help secure its place among perennial favorites. **ABOVE:** 'Voodoo,' AARS distinction in 1986, also smells of fruit, a sultry blend including something that will always be "rose." **AT LEFT:** 'Lagerfeld,' a 1986 grandiflora from America's Christensen, possesses a generous fragrance wrapped in a rare silvery-lavender color. It makes a perfect rose for cutting and loves to be seen by candlelight.

**OPPOSITE PAGE:** 'French Perfume,' a 1994 hybrid tea from the American firm Jackson & Perkins, bred by Suzuki, sets a high standard for big classic rose scent.

All four roses illustrated here have distinct meaning in the world of big, beautiful roses that smell like "roses" and all have been introduced since 1963. 'Tropicana' made its debut that year and caused a sensation. Not only was the plant vigorous and forthcoming with strong canes, the soon-to-open, high-centered buds turned into near glow-in-the-dark orange roses. It was a knock-

out to the eyes and since smelling couldn't be resisted, there was also a scent of ripe raspberries on a warm day, or was it the sun-ripened, homegrown apricots at Great Aunt Ella's? Since 'Tropicana' gave a favorable impression in all categories, it quickly became a modern classic of rose lovers.

'Lagerfeld' carries the glamour of the international fashion designer for whom it is named, not only for its automobile-world silveriness, hinting at blue, but a strong, sweet rose scent that some may say is assertive and masculine.

The name 'Voodoo' conjures dark mystery, but the rose by this name is full of fruity fragrance and comes in "trust-your-mother" colors, yellow, peach, orange, and later on, scarlet blushes. It won AARS in 1986, and has continued to earn a place in rose gardens. The dark green foliage resists disease and the exhibition-style flowers, with lots of big rose perfume, invite smelling in the garden or in a bouquet.

Not everyone who loves the smell of fresh roses will appreciate what that fragrance becomes after they are dried. It is quite possible, however, to dry roses that do give off a pleasant smell, or to preserve them in such a way that the petals, whole buds, and flowers, are things of beauty. Essential rose oil can be added to enhance the smell, or you can blend it with other fragrances, as you like. Dried roses look unusually appealing when set fairly close together, all of the same kind and color, in a flat bowl or straw basket.

Roses dry best in diffused light, out of direct sun, and in low humidity. Some colors dry beautifully, others fade but may still yield fragrance.

AT LEFT: 'Las Vegas'
is a modern hybrid
tea rose that can
succeed in show
business but may
require a personal
trainer to coax its
best performance.
Likewise, OPPOSITE
PAGE, 'Royal
Highness,' from
America's Swim,
1962, also responds
to special care.

# Exhibition

**GROWING ROSES THAT WIN** in competitions is a highly specialized activity that takes commitment and usually involves participation in local, regional, and national events sponsored by the American Rose Society. There are also roses considered at the top of their class for exhibition purposes that may not be particularly good or reliable garden roses. Exhibition is devoted to some of these possibilities. Each of the roses pictured is considered exceptionally beautiful, has a winning reputation as a show rose, and is cultivated passionately all over the world by individuals willing to do whatever is required to grow a rose beyond compare.

"Challenge class" is another way to look at this group of roses. All things being equal of course, some gardeners will find their easiest roses among these while others will understand perfectly. If a rose's unique set of needs happens to coincide with the grower's conditions and gardening style, only the challenge is lost. All else thrives!

Clearly, not every amateur rosarian who takes on the challenge of growing roses is destined to enter them into formal exhibitions. The greater number do aspire simply to achieve or exceed their personal best.

More often than not, growing an exhibition rose begins with fanatical preparation of the soil bed. Having chosen the most favored site possible, beds are typically dug out two feet deep and the piles of soil gotten thereby carted off, to be replaced by a near magical blending of a soil-less packaged planting medium such as Promix, well-rotted, composted manure, clean, sharp sand, perlite, and sphagnum peat moss.

This concoction assures a pathogen-free bed and drainage; for nutrients, see page 42.

Beds can be in almost any workable size; one that is four-and-a-half to five feet wide by 20 feet long will hold 20 rosebushes. In a good season these can yield an average of ten quality flowers per day, per bush—a lot!

Before or while planting the rosebushes, it is a wise plan to install an automatic drip irrigation system. This seeps water into the soil where it is needed, not up on the leaves where it might foster disease. The means of application is also efficient and helps maintain ideal moisture conditions at the root level: This consistency and steadiness produces strong, unhampered growth, lustrous foliage, and prodigious flowering. If your soil grows great vegetables, little amendment or digging is needed to grow superior roses as well.

40      *Exhibition*

OPPOSITE PAGE, CLOCKWISE FROM UPPER LEFT: 'Sun Goddess,' is a 1994 Warriner in classic exhibition form and slight scent. 'Wild Ginger,' 1976 grandiflora, came from a breeder named Buck and was introduced by Iowa State University. It has cold hardiness and puts forth a glorious flower. 'Fascination' hybrid tea, a 1982 Warriner, has slight fragrance but everything else that makes a great and unique rose. 'Bel Amis,' Laperriere's 1958 introduction, has a satiny perfection that soothes both eyes and souls. 'Dean Collins,' 1955 grandiflora, from breeder Lammerts has a slight fragrance and an unusually large flower, exceptional color in the garden or cut. The lightly tea-scented 'Sheer Elegance' (AARS 1991) came from Jerry Twoney, an amateur breeder.

THIS PAGE, CLOCKWISE FROM ABOVE: 'Early Morn,' a 1944 Brownell hybrid tea, has old-fashioned appeal and fragrance. 'Audrey Hepburn,' DeVor's 1992 hybrid tea, gives a moderately fruity fragrance. 'Headliner,' a 1985 Warriner hybrid tea, is beautiful at all stages, in the garden and in the home. 'Rochefort,' 1936 hybrid tea, is from Mallerin and fragrant.

ABOVE: 'Casanova' is a hybrid tea that can make it on its own yet with some extra TLC, it can produce exceptionally large roses for cutting.
AT RIGHT: 'Harry Wheatcroft,' named for the English rosarian and eccentric character who introduced it in 1972, is an appropriately "different" rose, a hybrid tea sport from 'Picadilly.' It has orange-red flowers streaked with a glowing yellow and slight scent.

Whether an exhibition or challenge-class rose is planted in garden soil or in a special soil-less, pathogen-free mix (see page 38), additional nutrients will be needed to boost its overall growth. A well-balanced diet produces a desirable quantity of buds that grow steadily to become perfect flowers with unblemished petals having a heavy, velvety texture and long life.

A standard fertilizing program proven for growing large-flowered hybrid tea roses in quantities for show is to make three applications per year of a mix comprised of one-third cup 38-0-0 slow-release nitrogen fertilizer, one-third cup alfalfa meal and pellets, and one-third cup 0-20-20. A cup of this mix is applied around each rosebush, raked, and watered three times a year: in spring, summer, and late summer, or approximately March-April, May-June, and July-early August.

Each rose grower learns by observation how to get the best results with a given rose. Some cultivars may prove inexplicably intolerant of local winters, by which the dedicated will not be defeated, only inspired to try again, by wintering the tender buds indoors in a pot, with grow lights.

Remember, it's possible to grow great roses with one spring application of all-season, timed-release fertilizer pellets. Steady nutrition pays.

# For Cutting

**YOU CAN GROW ROSES FOR CUTTING** in any convenient spot where their growing needs can be met. Many gardeners grow roses only to cut, hardly considering them as part of the garden proper. Or, roses known to perform well outdoors can be assigned that role and those favored for the production of cut flowers can grow in a practical place, in rows in the kitchen garden, for example, as illustrated on the opposite page at Pashley in rural England.

A rose cutting garden can also be made an appealing destination if it is set out in a formal plan with an evergreen or herb hedging such as dwarf boxwood, santolina, or germander. Add a wooden or iron bench under a lattice arbor bowered in climbing roses, and no one will guess this is primarily a factory for turning out perfect rosebuds and half-opened blossoms, ready to be cut with nice long stems early in the morning or late in the afternoon. Soon they will enliven the house.

While it may seem surprising, all things being equal, a rose will last somewhat longer cut and in a vase of fresh water than when left to its fate on the bush.

AT LEFT: 'Electron,' a 1970 Patrick McGredy from New Zealand, also known as 'Mullard Jubilee,' has strong rose-pink hybrid tea flowers with a light scent and is ideal as a bud-vase rose, from newly opening bud to fully open blossom. BELOW: 'Unforgettable,' a 1992 Warriner hybrid with a light rose scent, ages from a dark to a silvery pink and lasts longer cut than when left in the garden.

Use hand pruners in a design that will not crush the stem; Felco No. 6 pruning shears are the standard by which all others are judged, and are often considered the best friend of both rosarian and flower arranger. Carry a bucket of cool, clean water into the garden and immediately plunge each cut stem several inches deep.

Later, in the house, or in a shaded work spot outdoors, remove the lower leaves from along the stem, any that would be submersed into the bouquet or more formal arrangement. Recut, at a slanting angle, a half inch or so of stem, under water, then place immediately into a vase or other vessel of fresh, cool to room-temperature water.

Well-grown roses that are cut and conditioned with care will last for up to a week. They can be arranged and displayed in plain water, water with a preservative added (which slows the growth of harmful bacteria and prolongs cut flower life), inserted in pre-soaked florist foam, or placed in individual florist water picks for the lavish touch of fresh roses in a door wreath, wedding festoon, or other floral decoration.

As the life of a cut rose ends, some retain their petals, others drop them. Those that retain them can be bunched, tied, and hung as dried decorations in a protected place.

AT RIGHT: 'Pristine,' a 1978 Warriner, with pink-blushed white flowers and long, tapered buds, looks good alone, in its own bouquet, or in any mixture with other flowers. AT RIGHT, BOTTOM: 'Dynasty,' a 1991 Warriner, does not have a scent but makes up for it in the generosity of its long- stemmed, orange- and-yellow hybrid tea flowers.

If otherwise promising cut roses droop prematurely, they can often be resuscitated by submersing in cool water, for a few hours or overnight. In such cases, the bathtub is an excellent option, using stones or bricks to anchor them. This method works surprisingly well with florist or garden roses and can sometimes save the day from certain "droopy" disappointment.

Roses grown with a proper diet provide larger, stronger flowers that also last longer when cut. Besides, thorough soil preparation at planting time, combined with good moisture from rain or irrigation, lots of sun, fresh air, and balmy temperatures, making about three applications of fertilizer in each growing season also helps. Beginning usually in March-April, another application midway, late May-June, and a third and final, in July-early August will prolong the life of your roses. A known plan for producing large numbers of show quality cut roses is to mix together one-third cup 38-0-0 slow-release nitrogen fertilizer, one-third cup alfalfa meal and pellets, and one-third cup 0-20-20; apply around each bush, rake in, and water well.

If a fresh-picked rose wilts, revive it by recutting the stem and submerging it to its neck in cool water. Shade and coolness also helps.

## 'LOVE' CUT ROSES

I F PRESSED *to name a favorite rose, many individuals will say they love all the same, especially one or two or even three in a bud vase.*

*Or how about two or three hundred roses all the same or in flattering colors, cut to the same length and displayed as one? A recent style, developed internationally in the 1990s, is to cut the roses with short stems and to bunch them in rounds or squares — set out like the crown jewels on a table, accented with a low light to make them glow.*

AT RIGHT: A collection of all-white flowers stands waiting in a sink of cool, fresh water, before being put into arrangements and decorations. White roses are complemented by similarly white orchids, daisies, tulips, and freesia. Try them mixed or in separate bouquets.

Hardly any flower spells romance when cut like the tea rose. The baby and sweetheart ones are perfect for a tot's first floral gift or for working into a bride's bouquet—all white on white with stephanotis, baby's-breath, and sweet peas. Since roses come in nearly all colors, some clear or primary such as red and yellow, others pastel or even smoky, they are perfect for wedding and anniversary decorations. Often, they can be a source of inspiration for a color scheme that can be carried out in the bride's-maids' dresses, bouquets, and in the table linens and decorations for all events.

Roses intended for decorating an important event need to be picked a day or two in advance and conditioned in deep vases or buckets of water. By the time they are put into arrangements, bouquets, corsages, or festoons, the stems and flowers are saturated with water and will therefore be able to stand up well for the momentous occasion.

Usually the roses will be arranged in pre-soaked florist foam or inserted individually in florist water picks; designed not to leak, these contain a rubber cap with a hole in the center through which the end of the stem is thrust so they can drink.

Festoons of cut roses and greenery are a most romantic way to decorate a church or wedding-dinner tables and in this application, the pre-conditioned flowers may be hastily wired in place, along with the greenery, and positioned without benefit of florist foam or water picks. They will last for several hours or even overnight if the air is not too dry, overly-hot, or too chilly. If at all possible, cut roses early in the day, before they're affected by sun and heat.

When the party's over, the fresh bouquet starts to go. Fortunately, many cut roses can segue into another life merely by being bunched loosely, tied, and hung to dry in the open air.

**OPPOSITE:** 'Pristine,' with its tinge of pink blush, is the essence of the perfect wedding or anniversary rose.

**AT LEFT:** 'Bride's bouquet for Laura,' by the author, for the wedding of his elder son Mark. White tea rosebuds elegantly star in a setting of waxy, starry, perfumed stephanotis, baby carnations, baby's-breath and a ruffle of galax leaves. All flowers were preconditioned for a few hours, then inserted in a tiny florist water pick and combined with the others in the arrangement. They were kept cool, overnight, in the refrigerator, at about 42°F and now they're ready for the afternoon wedding the next day.

**OVERLEAF, LEFT:** 'Ingrid Bergman,' from Denmark's Poulsen, 1983, is superb cut and in a vase or, as here, laid to dry in a low basket. **RIGHT:** Roses can look as beautiful in a canning jar as in a proper vase. Recut stems and change vase water frequently to prolong the gorgeous blooms.

**ABOVE:** 'Princesse de Monaco' is from France's Meilland family, honoring Princess Grace and recalling another Meilland gift to the world, 'Peace.' Sumptuous pink-blushed roses give off a full-bodied, fruity rose fragrance. One great beauty honors another.

# Growing

**PRIMARY TO SUCCESS WITH ROSES IS** an abundance of water, sunlight, fresh air, nutrients, and, to sustain active growth, temperatures between 50° and 90°F. Most can survive winter lows of 0°F to far colder and so too can they withstand torrid summers and searing winds, where days can reach 100°F or more. Despite the distressing extremes, roses can quickly rebound when the going gets easier and reward their growers, in four to eight weeks, with high-centered, ever-so-hopeful buds. Given half a chance, these will unfurl into every promise of beauty.

Roses' need for water also means they require a well-drained site. Standing in water longer than overnight is not good. They will grow in almost any soil—clay, sand, or deep loam—provided excess moisture can drain off quickly.

Roses also respond vigorously to long-range soil improvement, primarily gained from annually side-dressing the bushes with generous portions of homemade garden compost. Spent mushroom compost is excellent as is well-rotted manure.

If you live in a climate given to many inches of annual rainfall, 35 to 40 inches or more, grow your roses in raised planting beds, at least eight to twelve inches above the endemic soil grade. In arid regions, berm the rose beds to catch water.

AT LEFT: Roses grow best in a place that receives at least a half day or more of sun and where the soil is free from the greedy roots of large trees and shrubs. The addition of a gazebo and comfortable outdoor furniture adds to the appeal of the rose garden in all seasons.

57

The healthier and more vital the soil, so too will be the rosebushes growing in it. No amount of fertilizer can take the place of soil that has been cultivated, spaded, forked, amended with a drainage enhancer, a humus-giver, or perhaps time-released fertilizer pellets, and in general fussed over rather than cursed at.

During much of the 20th century, the large-flowered hybrid tea roses have been associated with a reliance on pesticides to keep them healthy. Increasingly, home gardeners and hobbyists are switching to a more ecologically conscious policy of growing a dynamic soil that produces an inherently stronger rosebush and flower factory—without any dependency on the use of insecticides, miticides, fungicides, or all-purpose pesticides.

Roses can be stronger and more abundant in flowers if they have free air movement. This means planting at least a foot or so from solid walls, but also giving the rose, particularly if taller or climbing, the benefit of a hedgerow, or other shield, from strong, prevailing, perhaps seasonal winds. Deadheading also promotes bloom.

When all is said and done, nothing works for roses like well-drained soil enhanced with annual side dressings of homemade compost. Oh yes, add water and sun.

## HELPFUL HINTS

**S**HARP PRUNERS *that feel right to your hands will help you be a better and happier rose grower. Hand pruners, like the ones pictured here, can be used to cut wood up to the thickness of a pencil or about one-quarter inch. Use long-handled pruners, also called loppers, to remove old rose canes up to about three-quarters inch diameter. If larger, use a pruning saw. Thick, leather or heavy-duty gloves with gauntlet cuffs help*

*protect hands and forearms at pruning and planting time.*

*Raised planting beds will also add to the pleasure and success in growing tea roses. Salvaged logs from trees on the site can often be used to outline a bed, or 1 x 6 lumber can be installed for a more formal effect.*

*Enriched topsoil can be brought in and mixed with compost to help grow stronger, healthier and fuller rosebushes.*

**LEFT:** Refined tea roses complement a rustic shed. **ABOVE:** Tea roses grow beautifully in 12-inch or larger clay pots. Watering freely and consistently is the secret. **OVERLEAF:** Hybrid tea roses in April at a quaint bed and breakfast in Natchez, MS.

# RESOURCES

*Some North American Rosebush Suppliers & Specialists*

**Bridges Roses**
2734 Toney Road
Lawndale, NC 28090
704.538.9412; catalog $1

**W. Atlee Burpee & Co.**
300 Park Ave.
Warminster, PA 18974-0001
800.333.5808; catalog free

**Butner's Old Mill Nursery**
806 South Belt Highway
St. Joseph, MO 64507
816.279.7434; catalog free

**Carroll Gardens, Inc.**
444 East Main Street
P.O. Box 310, Westminster, MD 21158
410.848.5422; catalog $3

**Donovan's Roses**
P.O. Box 37800
Shreveport, LA 71133-7800
318.861.6693; catalog for SASE

**Hardy Roses of the North**
Box 9
Danville, WA 99121-0009
250.442.8442

**Hidden Springs Nursery**
170 Hidden Springs Lane
Cookeville, TN 38501;
catalog $1

**Historical Roses**
1657 West Jackson Street
Painesville, OH 44077
216.357.7270 (SASE for catalog)

**Hortico, Inc.**
723 Robson Rd.
Waterdown, ON L0R 2H1
Canada 905.689.6984;
catalog $3

**Interstate Nurseries**
1706 Morrissey Drive
Bloomington, IL 61704

**Jackson & Perkins Co.**
1 Rose Lane
Medford, OR 97501
1.800.USA.ROSE

**Kelly Nurseries**
410 8th Ave. N.W.
Faribault, MN 55021
507.334.1623

**Louisiana Nursery**
Route 7, Box 43
Opelousas, LA 70570
318.948.3696; catalog $6

**Lowe's Own-Root Roses**
6 Sheffield Road
Nashua, NH 03062;
catalog $2

**Mini-Rose Garden**
P.O. Box 203
Cross Hill, SC 29332
864.998.4331

**Moore Sequoia Nursery**
2519 E. Noble
Visalia, CA 83282
209.732.0190; catalog free

**Nor'East Miniature Roses, Inc.**
P.O. Box 307
Rowley, MA 01969
508.948.7964

**Northland Rosarium**
9405 S. Williams Lane
Spokane, WA 99224
E-mail cparton@ior.com

**Park Seed**
Cokesbury Road
Greenwood, SC 29647-0001
864.223.7333

**Pickering Nurseries, Inc.**
670 Kingston Road
Pickering, Ont. L1V 1A6
Canada
905.839.2111; catalog $4

**Plants of the Southwest**
Aqua Fria, Route 6,
Box 11A
Santa Fe, NM 87501;
catalog $3.50

**Rose Acres**
6641 Crystal Boulevard
El Dorado, CA 95623-4804
916.626.1722

**Roseraie at Bayfields, The**
P.O. Box R
Waldoboro, ME 04572
207.832.6330;
narrated video catalog $9

**Roses & Wine**
3528 Montclair Road
Cameron Park, CA 95682
916.677.9722

**Spring Hill Nurseries**
110 W. Elm Street
Tipp City, OH 45371

**Spring Valley Roses**
N7637 330th Street
P.O. Box 7
Spring Valley, WI 54767
715.778.4481

**Wayside Gardens**
1 Garden Lane
Hodges, SC 29695-0001
800.845.1124

**White Flower Farm**
P.O. Box 50
Litchfield, CT 06759-0050
800.503.9624; catalog $4

*Rose Society and Competitions*

**American Rose Society**
P.O. Box 3900
Shreveport, LA 71130-0030
318.938.5402

**All-America Rose Selections, Inc.**
221 N. LaSalle St., Suite 3900
Chicago, IL 60601
312.372.7090

---

### Metric Conversions
APPROXIMATE

| TEMPERATURE | | | | LENGTH | | |
|---|---|---|---|---|---|---|
| WHEN YOU KNOW | MULTIPLY BY | TO FIND | | WHEN YOU KNOW | MULTIPLY BY | TO FIND |
| °F / Fahrenheit temp. | 5/9 (-32) | Celsius temp. / c° | | in. / inches | 2.54 | centimeters / CM |
| °C / Celsius temp. | 9/5 (+32) | Fahrenheit temp. / F° | | ft. / feet | 30 | centimeters / CM |